To Celise
from the Judges
2009

AUSTRALIAN JOURNEY

Debra Doenges   Andrew Teakle

Dedication

From Debra: This book is dedicated to my loving parents, Milan and Lila Pelouch, whose individual talents in art and photography started me on my path.
From Andrew: This book is lovingly dedicated to my parents, Robert and Noela Teakle. You are the best people I know.

First published in Australia in 2007 by
New Holland Publishers (Australia) Pty Ltd
Sydney • Auckland • London • Cape Town

1/66 Gibbes Street Chatswood NSW 2067 Australia
218 Lake Road Northcote Auckland New Zealand
86 Edgware Road London W2 2EA United Kingdom
80 McKenzie Street Cape Town 8001 South Africa

Copyright © 2007 images as credited
Copyright © 2007 New Holland Publishers (Australia) Pty Ltd

Australian journey.

ISBN 9781741106251 (hbk.).

1. Landscape - Australia - Pictorial works. 2. Animals - Australia - Pictorial works. 3. Photography, Artistic. 4. Australia - Pictorial works. I. Doenges, Debra.

919.400222

Publisher: Fiona Schultz
Designer: Debra Doenges and Andrew Teakle
Production Manager: Linda Bottari
Printer: Tien Wah Press (Malaysia) Pte Ltd

10 9 8 7 6 5 4 3 2

Cover: Dawn Over Friendly Beach, Freycinet National Park, TAS, Andrew Teakle
Title page: Water-streaked Canyon Wall, Uluru-Kata Tjuta National Park, NT, Debra Doenges
Page 3: Cabbage Palms, Eungella National Park, QLD, Debra Doenges
Page 4: Ghost Gum, Devils Marbles, NT, Andrew Teakle

www.tesseraphoto.com   www.tesseratravel.com

Introduction

For local and international travellers alike, Australia offers a dazzling variety of experiences, and more than most people could enjoy in a lifetime. It is filled with seemingly endless sun-soaked beaches, seductive cities, primordial rainforests and the vast outback. Australian Journey will take you around this large, diverse, and majestic continent, filling the senses while providing an insight into Australia's character and beauty.

Starting in Sydney, these 126 photographs take you on a journey past Australia's capital, Canberra, through the Southern Alps and towards Melbourne. Jump across Bass Strait to the lush, temperate island of Tasmania. Back on the mainland, follow the Southern Ocean then head inland to the majestic Flinders Ranges and Lake Eyre before crossing the Nullarbor. Once over to the west, follow the coast north to the iconic Kimberley. Travel across the Top End, through Central Australia and down again along the Queensland coast before arriving just north of Sydney in the Hunter Valley.

Through these images we attempt to go beyond a recording of what a place looks like, which changes with the light, the season and the perspective. Our job as photographers is to be patient, to scour the area, hunting down a viewpoint that tells a story and transports you into a scene at its most captivating time. We wait, sometimes for days, or return years later, to encounter the best light and conditions so that we can, in turn, communicate the magical moment to you.

We hope you enjoy this journey around our homeland, and trust your own journey is full of wonder and joy.

OPERA HOUSE & HARBOUR BRIDGE
Sydney, NSW

Andrew Teakle

Debra Doenges

SUNSET WALK
Sydney Harbour Bridge, NSW

8

HYDE PARK
Sydney, NSW

Debra Doenges

9

Andrew Teakle

OCEAN BATHS AT COOGEE BEACH
Sydney, NSW

WAVES OVER TESSELLATED ROCK
Royal National Park, NSW

Andrew Teakle

Andrew Teakle

DAWN FROM PULPIT ROCK
Blue Mountains National Park, NSW

12

GRAND CANYON TRAIL
Blue Mountains National Park, NSW

Andrew Teakle & Debra Doenges

Andrew Teakle

FITZROY FALLS
Southern Highlands, NSW

BLACK SWANS IN MIST
Canberra, ACT

Debra Doenges

Debra Doenges

AUSTRALIAN WAR MEMORIAL
Canberra, ACT

16

SNOW GUMS & GRANITE
Kosciuszko National Park, NSW

Debra Doenges

Andrew Teakle

EMUS BESIDE THE MURRAY RIVER
Kosciuszko National Park, NSW

18

MT HOTHAM & RAZORBACK RIDGE
Alpine National Park, VIC

Andrew Teakle

Debra Doenges

AUTUMN VINEYARD
Bright, VIC

20

CRAIG'S HUT
Mt Stirling, VIC

Debra Doenges

Debra Doenges

MOUNTAIN ASH IN FOG
Yarra Ranges National Park, VIC

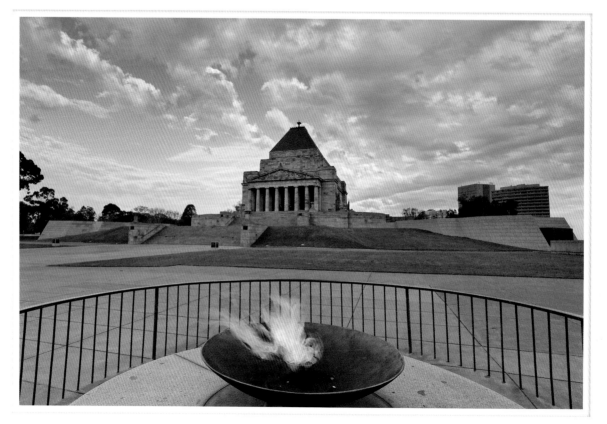

SHRINE OF REMEMBRANCE
Melbourne, VIC

Andrew Teakle

Andrew Teakle

BRIGHTON BATHING BOXES
Melbourne, VIC

SCULPTURE & SKYLINE
Melbourne, VIC

Andrew Teakle

Andrew Teakle

VICTORIAN ARTS CENTRE
Melbourne, VIC

DOVE LAKE & CRADLE MOUNTAIN
Cradle Mountain-Lake St Clair National Park, TAS

Andrew Teakle & Debra Doenges

27

Andrew Teakle & Debra Doenges

PANDANUS & DECIDUOUS BEECH IN SNOW
Cradle Mountain-Lake St Clair National Park, TAS

28

BLACK SWANS AT DAWN
Bruny Island, TAS

Andrew Teakle

29

Debra Doenges

DUSK OVER THE DERWENT RIVER
Hobart, TAS

DAWN OVER VICTORIA DOCK & MT WELLINGTON
Hobart, TAS

Debra Doenges

Debra Doenges

TREE FERNS & CREEK BED
Liffey Falls, TAS

32

TESSELLATED PAVEMENT
Tasman Peninsula, TAS

Debra Doenges

Debra Doenges

LICHEN ON GRANITE
Freycinet National Park, TAS

34

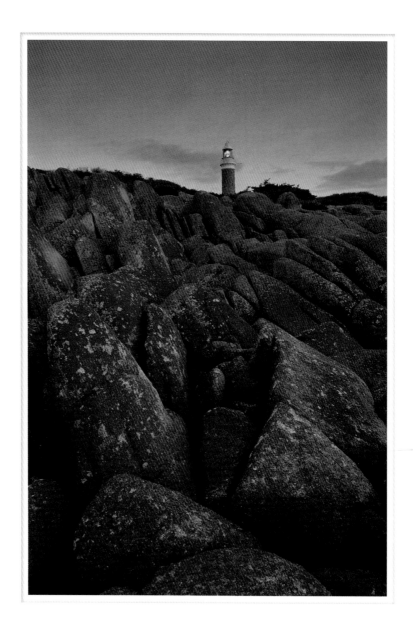

EDDYSTONE POINT LIGHTHOUSE   Andrew Teakle
Mt William National Park, TAS

Andrew Teakle

DAWN OVER HANSON BEACH
Port Campbell National Park, VIC

36

HOPETOUN FALLS
Otway Ranges, VIC

Andrew Teakle

Debra Doenges & Andrew Teakle

TURRETT FALLS
Grampians National Park, VIC

REMARKABLE ROCKS
Kangaroo Island, SA

Debra Doenges

Debra Doenges

VICTORIA SQUARE
Adelaide, SA

CONVENTION CENTRE & BLACK SWANS
Adelaide, SA

Debra Doenges

STOKES HILL LOOKOUT ▶
Flinders Ranges National Park, SA
Debra Doenges

42

SALT FLATS
Lake Eyre National Park, SA

Debra Doenges

Andrew Teakle

CAMEL, WOMBAT & KANGAROO
Nullarbor Plain, SA

44

SAND DUNES ALONG SOUTHERN OCEAN
Eucla National Park, WA

Debra Doenges

Andrew Teakle

CREEK'S END
Cape Le Grand National Park, WA

SALMON BEACH
Esperance, WA

Andrew Teakle

Debra Doenges

SAND & SKY
Fitzgerald River National Park, WA

48

GRASS TREES & BLUFF KNOLL
Stirling Ranges National Park, WA

Andrew Teakle

Andrew Teakle

FLINDERS PENINSULA
Torndirrup National Park, WA

RED TINGLE FOREST
Walpole-Nornalup National Park, WA

Debra Doenges

Debra Doenges & Andrew Teakle

SALMON BEACH WILDFLOWERS
D'Entrecasteaux National Park, WA

52

VINEYARD IN SPRING
Pemberton, WA

Debra Doenges

Debra Doenges

KARRI FOREST
Leeuwin-Naturaliste National Park, WA

RIVER MOUTH
Margaret River, WA

Andrew Teakle

55

Andrew Teakle

CANAL ROCKS
Yallingup, WA

SKYLINE AT DUSK
Perth, WA

Debra Doenges

Debra Doenges

KANGAROO SCULPTURE & MOSAIC
Perth, WA

THE PINNACLES
Nambung National Park, WA

Debra Doenges

Andrew Teakle

THE PINNACLES
Nambung National Park, WA

HOMESTEAD IN WHEAT FIELD
Geraldton, WA

Andrew Teakle

Andrew Teakle

RED BLUFF COAST
Kalbarri, WA

62

STROMATOLITES

Debra Doenges & Andrew Teakle

Shark Bay, WA

Andrew Teakle

SAND DUNE
Cape Range National Park, WA

64

SNAPPY GUM

Debra Doenges

Karijini National Park, WA

Andrew Teakle

OXERS LOOKOUT
Karijini National Park, WA

GANTHEAUME POINT
Broome, WA

Debra Doenges

Debra Doenges

BEEHIVE DOMES
Bungle Bungles, Purnululu National Park, WA

BOAB IN FOG
Parrys Lagoon, East Kimberley, WA

Debra Doenges

Debra Doenges

SANDSTONE CLIFFS
Hidden Valley, Mirima National Park, WA

PALM & EUCALYPT

Keep River National Park, NT

Andrew Teakle

Andrew Teakle & Debra Doenges

CANOEING KATHERINE GORGE

Nitmiluk National Park, NT

SUNSET OVER FANNIE BAY

Darwin, NT

Andrew Teakle

73

Debra Doenges

TOLMER FALLS
Litchfield National Park, NT

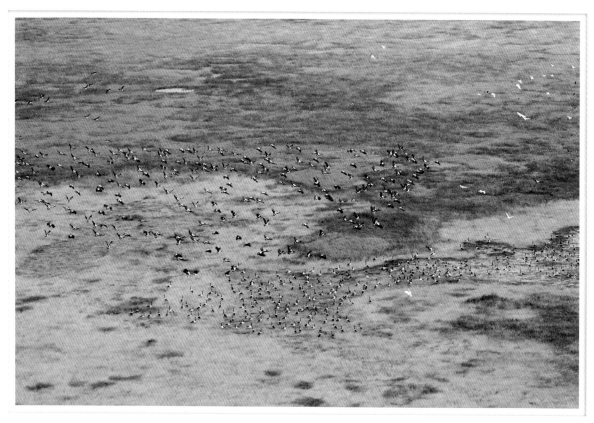

MAGPIE GEESE FLY OVER MAGELA WETLANDS
Kakadu National Park, NT

Andrew Teakle

Andrew Teakle

ROCK ART AT UBIRR
Kakadu National Park, NT

76

GHOST GUM AND BOULDERS
Devil Marbles, NT

Debra Doenges

Andrew Teakle

KALARANGA LOOKOUT
Finke Gorge National Park, NT

78

KINGS CANYON
Watarrka National Park, NT

Andrew Teakle

Debra Doenges

STORM CLOUDS OVER KATA TJUTA

Uluru-Kata Tjuta National Park, NT,

ULURU & HONEY GREVILLEA   Andrew Teakle

Uluru-Kata Tjuta National Park, NT

Debra Doenges

WINTER RAINS ON ULURU
Uluru-Kata Tjuta National Park, NT

82

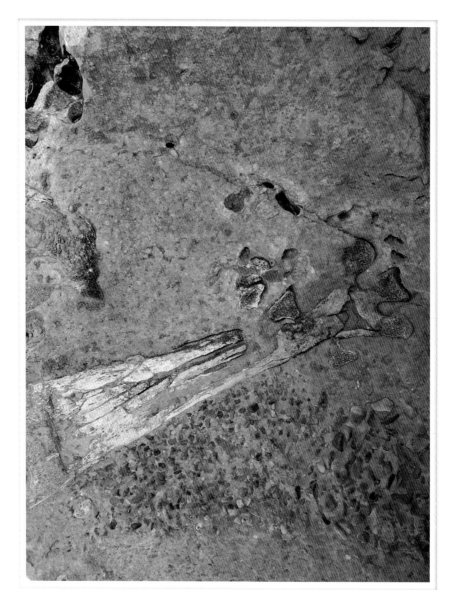

THUNDERBIRD FOSSIL
Riversleigh, QLD

Andrew Teakle & Debra Doenges

83

Debra Doenges

CATHEDRAL FIG TREE
Atherton Tablelands, QLD

ROCK WALLABY
Granite Gorge, Atherton Tablelands, Qld

Debra Doenges

85

Debra Doenges

ARLINGTON REEF
Great Barrier Reef, QLD

THE LAGOON
Cairns, QLD

Andrew Teakle & Debra Doenges

Debra Doenges & Andrew Teakle

SOUTH COWIE BEACH
Daintree National Park, QLD

FAN PALM RAINFOREST
Daintree National Park, QLD

Debra Doenges

Debra Doenges

CAPE TRIBULATION
Daintree National Park, QLD

Andrew Teakle

ROSE DAWN
◀ Mission Beach, QLD
Debra Doenges

WATERVIEW CREEK
Jourama Falls, Paluma Range National Park, QLD

92

SUNSET STORM
Townsville, QLD

Debra Doenges

Debra Doenges

ALLIGATOR CREEK REFLECTIONS
Bowling Green Bay National Park, QLD

MURRAY BAY & GLOUCESTER ISLAND   Debra Doenges
Bowen, QLD

Debra Doenges

HILL INLET
Whitsunday Islands, QLD

HAYMAN ISLAND
Whitsunday Islands, QLD

Debra Doenges & Andrew Teakle

Debra Doenges

TULIP OAK BLOSSOMS ON FAN PALM

Eungella National Park, QLD

BROOMFIELD REEF   Andrew Teakle
Capricorn Coast, Great Barrier Reef, QLD

Debra Doenges

MOSS GARDEN
Carnarvon Gorge National Park, QLD

DAWN OVER WILD CATTLE CREEK

Debra Doenges

Tannum Sands, QLD

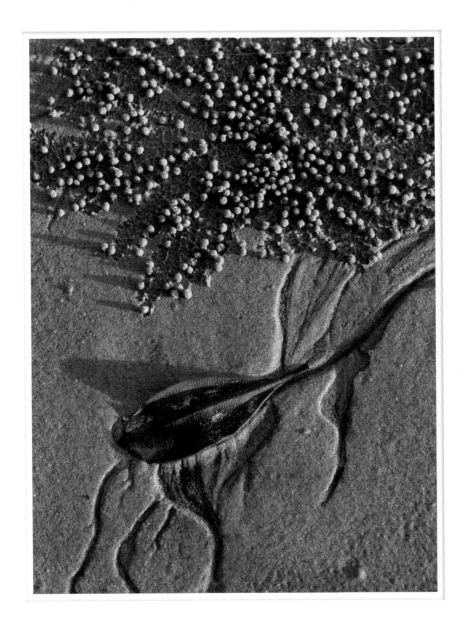

Debra Doenges

CRAB PATTERNS & AUTUMN LEAF
Town of 1770, QLD

HUMPBACK WHALE TAIL
Hervey Bay, QLD

Andrew Teakle

Debra Doenges

LAKE ALLOM
Fraser Island, Great Sandy National Park, QLD

MAHENO SHIPWRECK
Fraser Island, Great Sandy National Park, QLD

Andrew Teakle & Debra Doenges

Debra Doenges

SUNRISE OVER TEEWAH BEACH
Cooloola Coast, Great Sandy National Park, QLD

PELICAN
Noosa Beach, QLD

Andrew Teakle

107

Andrew Teakle

GLASS HOUSE MOUNTAINS
Sunshine Coast Hinterland, QLD

RIVERFIRE OFF THE STORY BRIDGE
Brisbane, QLD

Debra Doenges

Andrew Teakle

BOUGAINVILLEA ARCHWAY
Southbank, Brisbane, QLD

CITY CAT ON THE BRISBANE RIVER
Brisbane, QLD

Andrew Teakle

Debra Doenges

CARNIVAL OF FLOWERS
Toowoomba, QLD

112

BALANCING ROCK
Girraween National Park, QLD

Debra Doenges

Debra Doenges

SUNFLOWERS
Clifton, QLD

SURFERS PARADISE
Gold Coast, QLD

Debra Doenges

Debra Doenges

BOOGEY BOARDING
Burleigh Heads, Gold Coast, QLD

Andrew Teakle

KINGSCLIFF BEACH
Tweed Coast, NSW

MOUNT LINDSAY SUNSET
◀ Gold Coast Hinterland, QLD
Debra Doenges

SEA EAGLE
Tallow Beach, Byron Bay, NSW

Debra Doenges

Andrew Teakle

CAPE BYRON LIGHTHOUSE
Byron Bay, NSW

BANKSIA IN FOG
New England National Park, NSW

Andrew Teakle

 121

Debra Doenges

Guy Fawkes River National Park, NSW

122

VEE WALL
Nambucca Heads, NSW

Debra Doenges

Debra Doenges

WHITE-BREASTED WOODSWALLOWS
Hat Head National Park, NSW

124

SUNSET OVER DIAMOND HEAD
Crowdy Bay National Park, NSW

Debra Doenges

Andrew Teakle

MELALEUCA TREE
Bombah Broadwater, Myall Lakes National Park, NSW

DARK POINT
Myall Lakes National Park, NSW

Andrew Teakle

Debra Doenges

BOGEY HOLE OCEAN BATH
Newcastle, NSW

VINEYARD STORM
Hunter Valley, NSW

Andrew Teakle